TABLE OF CONTENTS

This book is dedicated to the memory of Kristin G. Jackson, a talented illustrator who was part of the TDAC Family from the very beginning and is greatly missed. Kristin's recipe is on page 42.

fig & grape shake

4 cups red grapes
1 cup fresh figs, stems removed
½ cup filtered water
½ tsp. vanilla extract
⅛ tsp. cinnamon
pinch of salt
2 cups ice cubes

Dried
2 OZ (5 FIGS)

Soak It

Chop It

Sliced & Frozen

MAPLE SYRUP
.5 FL OZ (1TBS)

Add It

Fig Banana Smoothie

4

APPLE JUICE

8 FL OZ (1 CUP)

Smoothie✱izer

2 servings

Blend It

✱ Serve It!

DUCCIO'S SPICY
FIG MARMELLATA

- 2 KG. - PEELED FIGS
- 2 TBS. CHILI PEPPER ★
- 50 GR. - PINOLI
- 100 GR. - PEELED ALMONDS
- 1 KG. SUGAR

★ DELICIOUS WITH CHEESE

put the chili pepper
and turn off the gas

5

peel 2 kg of figs

1

with sugar
for 12 hours
in the fridge

SUGAR

2

cook until the mass
decrease to 2/3,
for 35-50 min

3

cook for other 10 min
almonds   pinoli

4

Cali Sunshine →

California
FIGS
Strawberry
Fig Jam

1½ cups mashed strawberries
15 Dried figs, chopped finely
½ cup Sugar
¼ cup lime Juice
¼ cup water

Combine ingredients in heavy-bottom pot. **Heat** on medium-high. Bring to boil. Reduce heat to medium and Cook **12** mins, stirring. **Mash** to blend. When thick bubbles form, remove from heat. While still **Warm, Pour** into **Sterilized** jars. Cool completely before Storing in fridge.

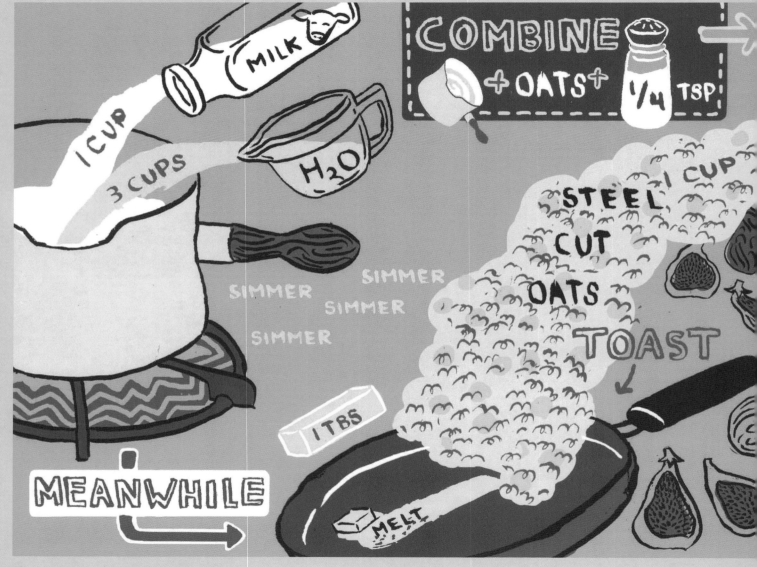

STIR UNTIL OATMEAL **THICKENS**

FOR FIGGY GLAZE HEAT

1 CUP DRIED FIGS

QUARTERED AND STEMMED

1/8 TSP

1/8 TSP

1 1/2 TBS H2O

1 1/2 TSP

OATMEAL WITH **HONEYED FIGS**

TOP WITH BROWN SUGAR

OATMEAL WITH HONEYED FIGS by Jessica McGuirl from Providence, RI (firstpancakestudio.com)   11

figs with sesame sauce

(1) Slice fresh, ripe figs any way you like

(2) Blend
   2 Tablespoons... sesame seed
   2 Tablespoons... water
   1 Tablespoon... vinegar
   1 Tablespoon... sugar
   ½ teaspoon corn starch

(3) Drizzle sesame sauce over figs and serve.

CARROTS & FIGS

INGREDIENTS:

- 1/4 cup slivered almonds
- 4 teaspoons sugar
- 1/2 teaspoon grated orange peel
- 1 pound carrots, cut into 1/4-inch slices
- 1/2 cup dried California figs, quartered
- 1 teaspoon butter or margarine, softened

PROCEDURE:

Cook almonds, sugar and orange peel in 8-inch skillet over low heat about 10 minutes stirring constantly, until sugar is melted and almonds are coated; cool. Break almonds apart; set aside.

Steam carrots in basket over boiling water for 9 to 11 minutes or until tender; add figs during last 2 minutes.

Toss carrots and figs with almonds and butter. Serve.

Serves: 4

Stuffed Figs

figs

prosciutto

goat cheese

honey

① cut figs in half

② stuff

③ wrap

④ drizzle

⑤ broil until bubbly and delicious!

After School Fig Bars

FIG BAR RECIPE

- COMBINE FIGS, SUGAR, WATER AND LEMON JUICE. COOK AND STIR OVER MEDIUM HEAT UNTIL THICK AND JAM-LIKE. SET ASIDE AND COOL.

- COMBINE BUTTER, BROWN SUGAR, EGGS, AND VANILLA IN A BOWL. BEAT TOGETHER WELL.

- STIR IN FLOUR, BAKING SODA, SALT, MIXING UNTIL SMOOTH.

- TURN DOUGH ONTO HEAVILY FLOURED SURFACE AND KNEAD A FEW TIMES TO A SMOOTH BALL.

- WITH A FLOURED ROLLING PIN, ROLL DOUGH TO A 14×12 INCH RECTANGLE.

- CUT LENGTHWISE INTO 4 STRIPS. SPOON FILLING EVENLY DOWN CENTER OF EACH STRIP.

- USE SPATULA TO TURN IN SIDES OF EACH STRIP TO ENCLOSE FILLING, BRING EDGES TOGETHER ON TOP OF FILLING AND PRESS TO SEAL.

- TURN SEAM SIDE DOWN AND CUT EACH STRIP CROSSWISE INTO 10 PIECES.

- ARRANGE ON GREASED BAKING SHEET AND BAKE AT 375° FOR 10-12 MINUTES, OR FIRM TO TOUCH.

Ingredients (illustrated):
- 2 CUPS CHOPPED DRIED FIGS
- 1/2 CUP SUGAR
- 3/4 CUP WATER
- JUICE OF 1 LEMON
- 1/2 CUP BUTTER
- 1 CUP BROWN SUGAR
- 2 EGGS
- 1 TEASPOON VANILLA
- 2 1/2 CUPS FLOUR
- 1/4 TEASPOON BAKING SODA
- 1/2 TEASPOON SALT

Fresh Fig & Avocado Salsa

2 jalapeno peppers

Remove seeds and ribs from peppers and slice very thin crosswise

1¾ ℗ diced California fresh figs

1 tbsp fresh lime juice

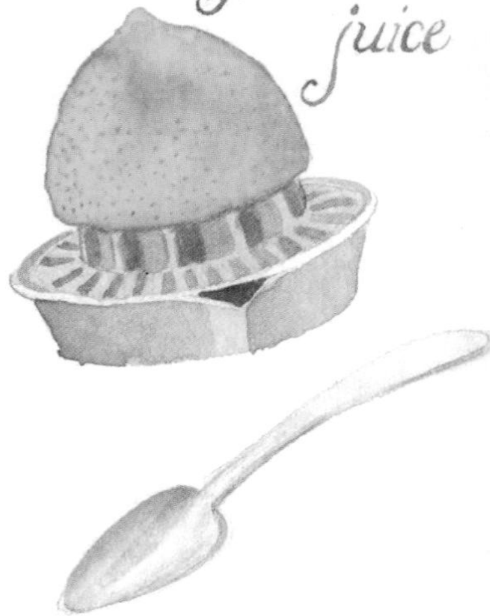

1 firm ripe avocado diced

¼ tsp salt

2 tbsp granulated sugar

½ tsp ground coriander

½ tsp ground cumin

¼ tsp garlic powder

Combine all ingredients in a bowl
Mix to blend well. Chill for several hours.

INGREDIENTS

2 cups fresh firm-ripe California figs, stemmed and diced
2 fresh green onions, sliced crosswise
2 medium tomatoes; peeled, seeded and coarsely chopped
1 cup peeled and diced mango
2 tablespoons finely chopped mint
2 cloves garlic, minced
2 jalapeno peppers, seeded and minced
2 teaspoons grated lime peel
2 tablespoons lime juice
1 tablespoon balsamic vinegar
salt and pepper to taste

PROCEDURE

Combine all ingredients and chill several hours to blend flavors.

"..the secret of my beauty.."

fresh FIGS salad, arugula and gorgonzola

INGREDIENTS:

1 teaspoon lemon juice

2 tablespoon extravirgin olive oil

1/2 teaspoon fresh ground black pepper

1/2 teaspoon salt

6 cups trimmed arugula (about 6 ounces)

8 fresh figs, each cut in fourth

1/4 cups gorgonzola crumbled

PROCEDURE:

Combine first 4 ingredients in a large bowl

add figs

add arugula

top with cheese

Serve immediately!

FRESH FIGS SALAD by Barbara Voarino from Turin, Italy (barbaravoarinodesigner.it) 25

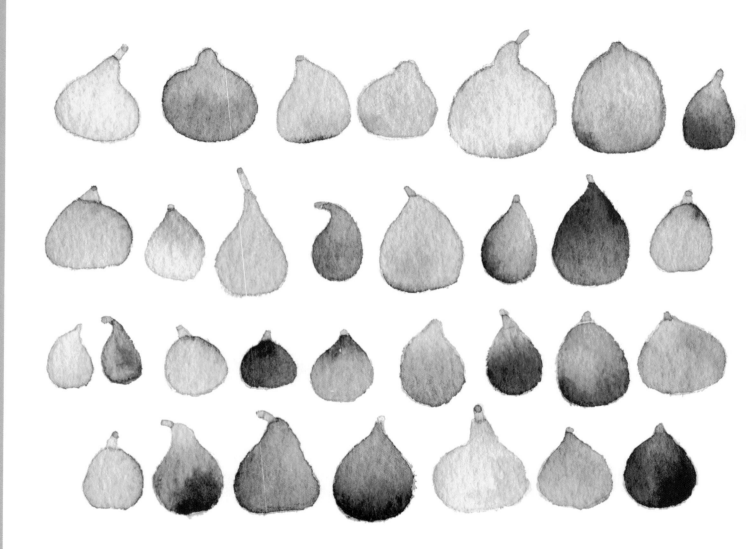

CARMELIZED FIG SALAD with CHEVRE and WALNUTS

This salad is decadently rich and surprisingly simple to make. Take a handful (or two) of mesclun salad greens. Place in bowl. Add about half a cup of walnuts, lightly toasted. Be careful not to burn them! Sprinkle a liberal amount of good CHEVRE (goat cheese) on top. Dress with a BASIC VINAGRETTE. Set aside. Now, the FUN PART. Take 8 FRESH FIGS, sliced in half and coated in OLIVE OIL. Place face up on a BROILER pan, and under the BROILER. Wait, watch and then remove once the figs begin to ooze sugary deliciousness. You'll know when.

Toss HOT FIGS with salad. The chevre will melt, covering the greens with runny, molten goat cheese and carmelized fig. Enjoy!

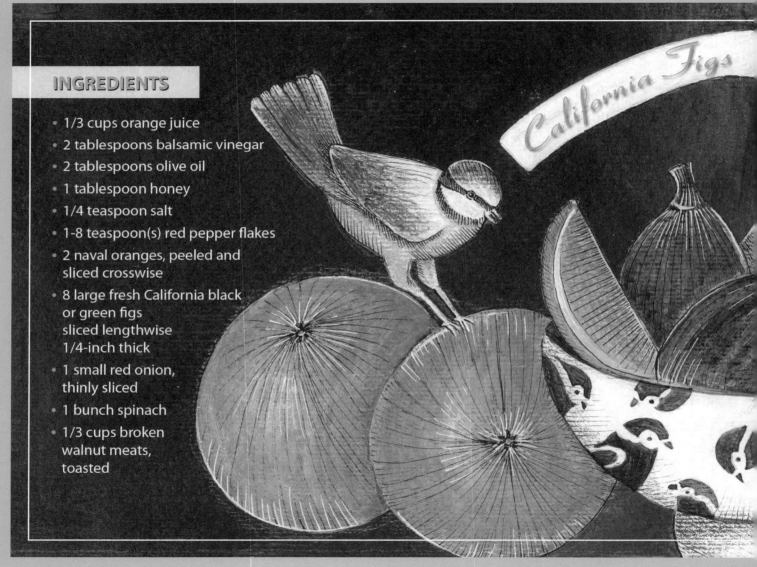

INGREDIENTS

- 1/3 cups orange juice
- 2 tablespoons balsamic vinegar
- 2 tablespoons olive oil
- 1 tablespoon honey
- 1/4 teaspoon salt
- 1-8 teaspoon(s) red pepper flakes
- 2 naval oranges, peeled and sliced crosswise
- 8 large fresh California black or green figs sliced lengthwise 1/4-inch thick
- 1 small red onion, thinly sliced
- 1 bunch spinach
- 1/3 cups broken walnut meats, toasted

California Figs

and Citrus Salad

PROCEDURE

To make dressing, combine juice, vinegar, oil, honey, salt and pepper flakes in blender container. Blend until thoroughly mixed. Place fruit and onion in large mixing bowl. Pour dressing over all. Set aside at least 10 minutes or up to one hour.

To serve: line individual salad plates with spinach leaves. Spoon fruit and dressing mixture on top, dividing equally. Sprinkle each salad with about 1 tbs toasted walnuts.

Enjoy your meal!

& figs

stRawBeRRies mix

it's so very simple
very very simple and attractive

TOSS TOGETHER all ingredients in a large bowl

Salad

ingredients:

handful of fresh strawberries

6 fresh figs sliced

elder or agave syrup

2 tbsp balsamic vinegar

FIGS & SALAMI FOCACCIA
(MY MOM'S PASSION)

1/2 CUP — OLIVE OIL

WATER — 1 1/2 CUP

5 tsp. — BREWER'S YEAST

3 tsp. SALT

MANITOBA FLOUR — 5 CUPS

2 tsp. SUGAR

IN A MIXING BOWL DISSOLVE THE SALT
IN WARM WATER AND ADD SUGAR,
8 TSP OF OLIVE OIL AND HALF FLOUR
AND MIX UNTIL THE BATTER IS SMOOTH AND LIQUID.
ADD THE CRUMBLED YEAST, KNEAD FOR 2-3 MINUTES.
ADD THE OTHER HALF OF THE FLOUR
AND KNEAD AGAIN FOR A FEW MINUTES.
POUR 1/4 CUP OF OLIVE OIL IN A RECTANGULAR PAN,
PLACE THE DOUGH AND BRUSH WITH OIL.
LET RISE FOR AN HOUR AND A HALF.
THEN ROLL OUT THE DOUGH
(LEAVING THE GROOVES WITH YOUR FINGERS),
BRUSH IT WITH OIL AND SPRINKLE WITH SALT.
LET RISE AGAIN FOR AN HOUR
AND BAKE THE FOCACCIA FOR 15 MINUTES
IN PREHEATED OVEN AT 390° F
(DO NOT OPEN THE OVEN DURING COOKING).
ALLOW TO COOL AND THEN CUT INTO RECTANGLES.

FOUR FIGS CUTIN HALF

A FEW SLICES OF SALAMI

FETTUCCINE + FIGS IN A BUTTER BALSAMIC SAUCE

Quarter 10 figs and toss them with 1 tablespoon olive oil.

Bake in shallow dish at 375° for 10 minutes.

Sauté 1 stick butter with ¼ cup good balsamic vinegar until reduced by half.

Add baked figs to the pan and sauté 1-2 minutes more.

Cook 1 pound fresh fettuccine.

In large bowl combine pasta, balsamic/butter/fig mix and 1 tablespoon poppy seeds.

SERVE IT UP!

maybe serve with a simple arugula salad and a nice pinot grigio

quinoa with figs and goat cheese

1 cup quinoa
2 figs
50 grams goat cheese
2 tablespoons honey
2 tablespoons pistachios
rose petals for serving

Preheat oven to 180c. Place figs in a small over proof dish and cut a cross section on top of each fruit. Open fig and place goat cheese into the cut. Drizzle with honey & back for 10-15 minutes.

While figs are in the oven cook the quinoa. Drain out any extra liquid.

Sprinkle the figs with chopped pistachios and spoon over any extra honey. Place figs on top and sprinkle with rose petals.

CHICKEN & figs ROLL

chicken... bacon... dried figs

roll 'em up together

toothpick

onions

salt

pepper

herbs

olive oil

200°C

45min

YUM!

GRILLED SCALLOPS & FIG KEBABS

COMBINE:

1/4 cup chopped green onions

1 large garlic clove, chopped

2 tbls low-sodium soy sauce

1/2 tsp ground red pepper

3 tbls orange marmalade

In a plastic bag, seal and -SHAKE-!!!

+ADD

12 ounces of sea scallops to the bag

SEAL

and allow to marinade for 20 minutes in the refrigerator

REMOVE Scallops from bag, reserving marinade

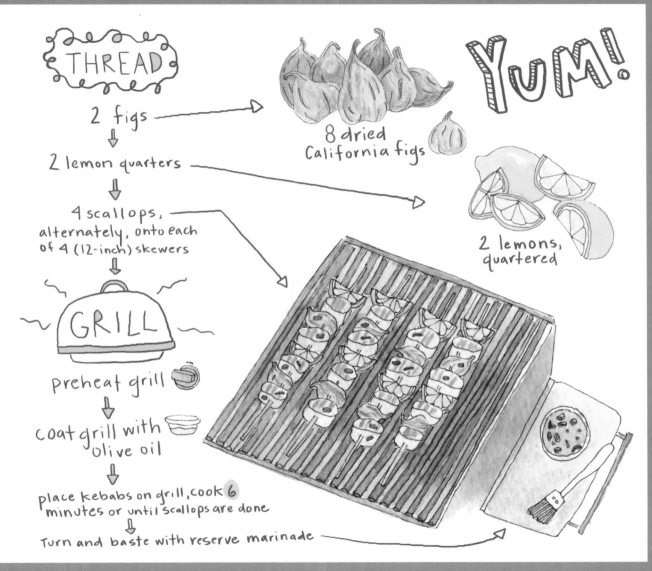

THREAD

2 figs

⬇

2 lemon quarters

⬇

4 scallops, alternately, onto each of 4 (12-inch) skewers

⬇

GRILL

preheat grill

⬇

coat grill with olive oil

⬇

place kebabs on grill, cook 6 minutes or until scallops are done

⬇

Turn and baste with reserve marinade

8 dried California figs

2 lemons, quartered

YUM!

Nonna's

What You Need:
6 figs
4 tbsp olive oil
2 tbsp brown sugar
1 cup mascarpone cheese
1/4 cup confectioner's sugar
mint leaves

brown sugar figs

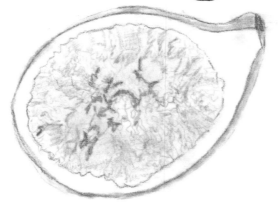

Figs are

Gluten-Free

What You Do:

Mix mascarpone with confectioner's sugar and set aside. Cut figs in half and put in bowl. Coat well with olive oil and brown sugar. Spear figs on skewers. Grill on medium high until figs caramelize and have marks on both sides. Plate figs, add dollop of cheese and top with mint leaves. Serve immediately!

Sarah Platanitis

1

12 inch pizza pan   +   1 pkg (18 oz.) sugar cookie dough at room temp

1/2 inch thick

1/4 inch thick

roll out dough with lightly floured hands.

2

325°

bake for 10 minutes until light brown, then cool.

combine and beat until smooth

1/4 c. marscapone [or sour cream]   +   1 egg   =

3

4 oz. cream cheese

4

spread over crust except for edges.   bake for 15-20 min. or until the filling is set & light brown. cool.

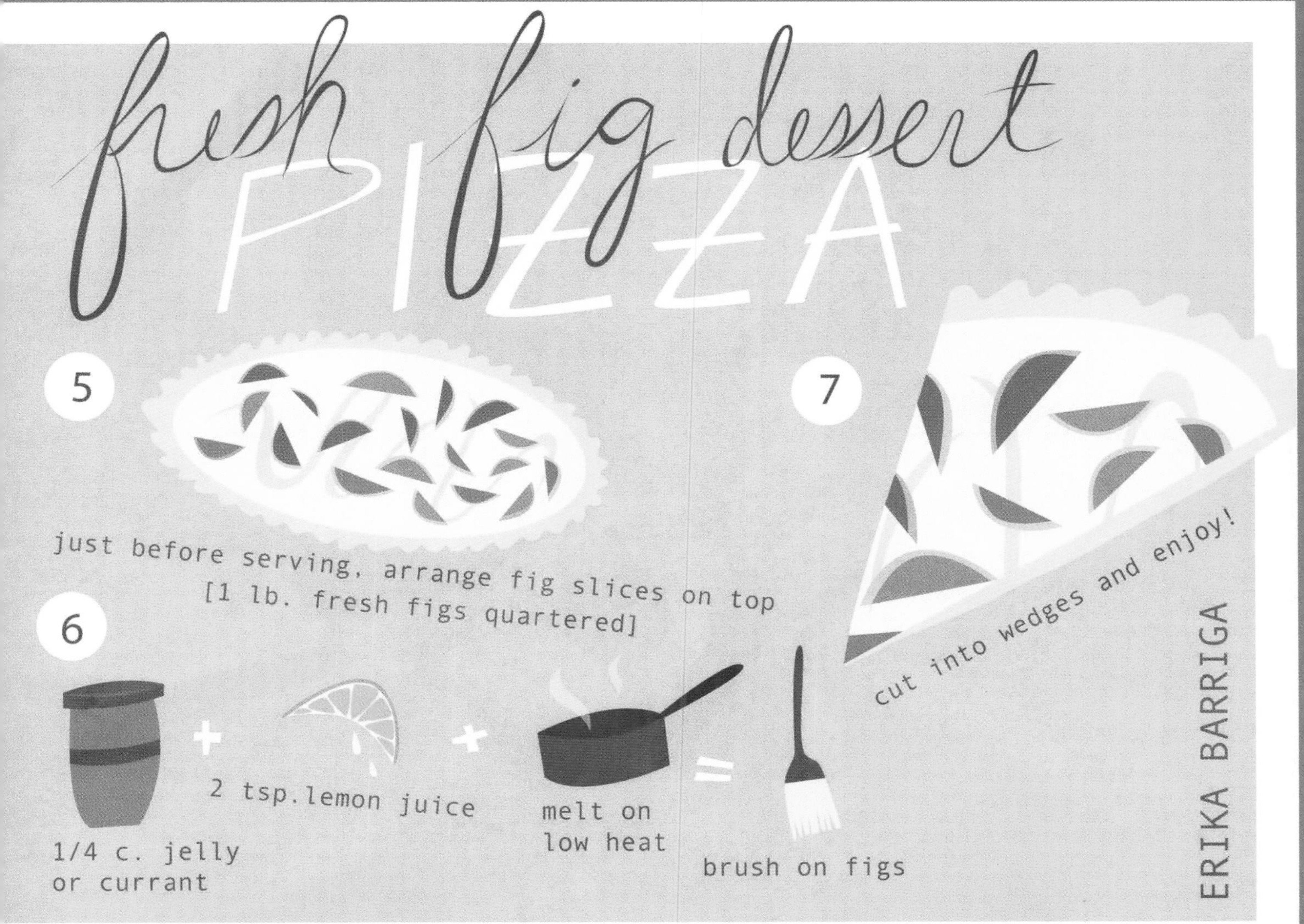

fresh fig dessert PIZZA

5

just before serving, arrange fig slices on top
[1 lb. fresh figs quartered]

6

1/4 c. jelly
or currant

+

2 tsp. lemon juice

+

melt on
low heat

=

brush on figs

7

cut into wedges and enjoy!

ERIKA BARRIGA

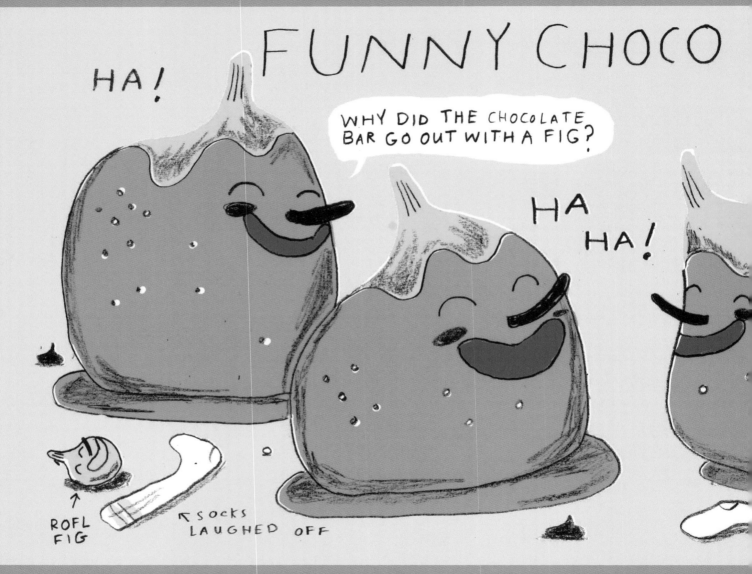

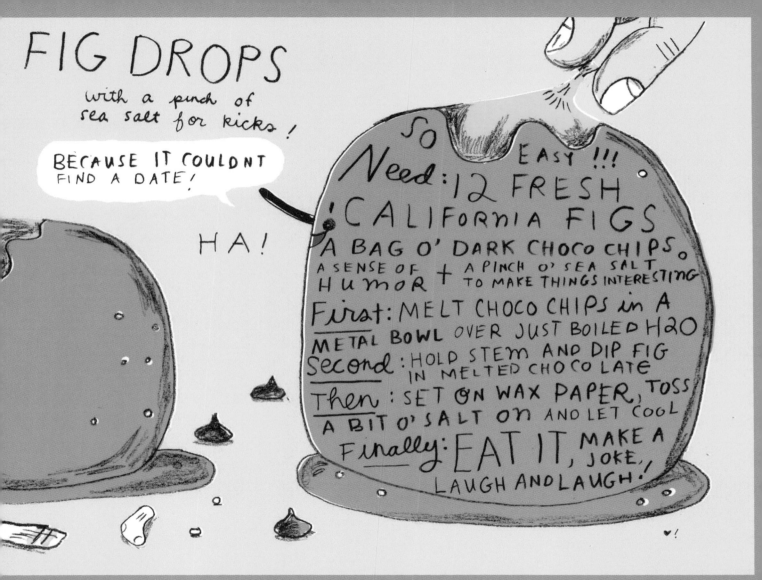

Tempting Fig and Apple CRISP

1 package dried figs, quartered

3 Tablespoons fruit juice

3 large apples, peeled, quartered
and sliced....

1/2 cup flour   1/2 cup oats

3/4 tsp. cinnamon   3/4 tsp. nutmeg

2/3 cup packed brown sugar

1/2 cup softened butter

Heat oven to 350 °.
Grease 8x8" baking dish
with cooking spray.
Place figs and fruit juice in
bowl; cover and microwave on
HIGH for 2 minutes. Let stand
for 5 minutes. Stir and set aside.

Arrange figs over sliced
apples in greased dish.
Mix remaining ingredients;
sprinkle over figs
and apples.
Bake until topping is golden
brown and filling is tender,
about 35 - 40 minutes.

Serve warm...
delicious with
ice cream!

Figs with Almonds

1 — Pick the figs when they are well ripen

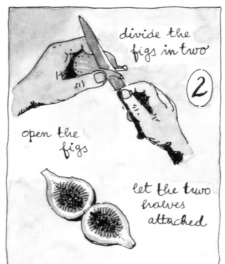

2 — divide the figs in two

open the figs

let the two halves attached

3 — August: the blue sky, the sun and the hot temperature will dry the figs in 6-7 days

(don't worry about insects or bees)

reed mat →

don't forget to turn figs every day

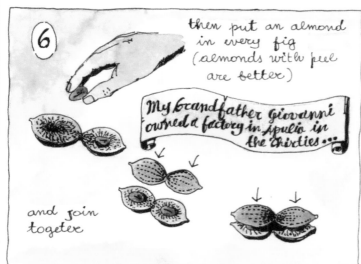

6 — then put an almond in every fig (almonds with peel are better)

My grandfather Giovanni owned a factory in Apulio in the thirties...

and join together

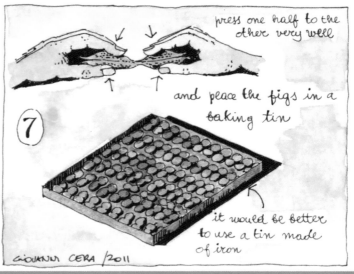

7 — press one half to the other very well

and place the figs in a baking tin

it would be better to use a tin made of iron

GIOVANNI CERA /2011

54

Don't let the figs outside at night or in rainy days!
When figs are dried they show yellow-brown color and have a typical good scent!
Then you need:

④

crushed cinnamon

baked almonds (one for every figs)

lemon Zest

chocolate powder (without sugar)

soak figs in the cinnamon ...

⑤

then in the chocolate

and in the chopped lemon Zest

Old Apulian recipe

bake them for 1/2 hour at 150°C ...

⑧

...and after having baked them...

when still boiling

⑨

press the figs togeter and let them cool.
Preserve them well pressed in a wicker basket

... and sent figs with almonds to Italians in Brooklyn too!!!

They will be a delicious dessert at Christmas time. Bey!!!

California figs
FLAMBE

Ingredients:

- ★ **12** fresh FIGS
- ★ 1/2 cup SUGAR
- ★ 1/2 cup WATER
- ★ **3** tablespoon fine granulated sugar

- ☆ **1/2** cup BRANDY
- ☆ whipped CREAM for topping

Put 12 fresh figs in the top pan, or blazer, of a chafing dish with 1/2 cup each of sugar and water, boiled together for 5 minutes

Put the pan over the heat until the figs and syrup are heated thru.

Sprinkle the figs with about 3 Tbs fine granulated sugar and pour over them 1/2 cup warmed brandy. Ignite the spirit and let the flame die. Serve the figs topped with whipped cream.

www.ilariaguarducci.blogspot.com

tonight

Evidently these three figs don't know what's happened to the other twelve...

ROBIN'S FIG TART

MAKE PRE-BAKED CRUST
CREAM 1 STICK UNSALTED BUTTER. MIX IN 1 c. POWDERED SUGAR, 1¾ c. FLOUR AND 1 EGG. DIVIDE INTO 2 BALLS, WRAP IN PLASTIC AND CHILL 2 HRS. (YOU CAN MAKE THE FILLING BELOW IN THE MEANTIME) THEN ROLL OUT 1 BALL. PRESS INTO TART PAN. TRIM EXCESS. CHILL 20 MINS. THEN BAKE AT 325° FOR 15-20 MINS. OR TIL EVENLY GOLDEN.

ALMOND CREAM FILLING
GRIND 2 c. SLIVERED ALMONDS WITH 1¼ c. GRANULATED SUGAR. BEAT 2 STICKS UNSALTED BUTTER WITH 1 c. SUGAR. COMBINE THE 2 IN A BOWL. ADD 2 EGGS AND 1 YOLK ONE AT A TIME. BEAT TIL LIGHT AND FLUFFY. SPREAD INTO COOLED CRUST.

PURÉE LAYER
REMOVE STEMS FROM 6 FRESH FIGS. PUREE THEM IN A FOOD PROCESSOR AND LAYER THIS OVER THE ALMOND CREAM FILLING.

FRUIT LAYER
QUARTER 12 FRESH FIGS AND ARRANGE SKIN SIDE DOWN OVER THE PURÉE. BAKE 30 MINS. AT 325° OR UNTIL FILLING IS GOLDEN. COOL 10 MINS. BRUSH WITH GLAZE.

LAST, GLAZE
WARM ¼ c. APRICOT JAM, THEN PUSH THROUGH SIEVE TO REMOVE PIECES. BRUSH TART WITH GLAZE.

*IF YOU'RE OUT OF FIGS...

...COULD BE PEACHES

...COULD BE PLUMS

...COULD BE APRICOTS

JACKIE CLARK MANCUSO

BRING ME SOME FIGGY PUDDING

BY NATE PADAVICK

8 FILL
8 RAMEKINS TO 50-75%

1 C.

*GREASE EACH WITH BUTTER FIRST!

9

BAKE 30 MIN

...WHILE YOU ARE WAITING MAKE THE SAUCE →→→

HEAVY WHIPPING **CREAM**
1 C.
1/8 TS SEA SALT
BROWN **SUGAR**
4 TBS BUTTER
3/4 C.
1 TBS **VANILLA**
*ADD THIS AT MINUTE 9

10 WHISK FOR 10 MIN
MED-LOW HEAT

11
COOL 10 MIN

12
CUT A CROSS

13 POUR THE SAUCE

14
SERVE WITH ICE CREAM AND HALF A FRESH FIG

THE END.

THEY DRAW & COOK.™

LET'S GET FIGGY: 30 Illustrated Fig Recipes Created by Artists from Around the World

Conceived, designed and produced by Studio SSS, LLC

STUDIO SSS, LLC
Nate Padavick & Salli Swindell
studiosss.tumblr.com

To see over 5,000 more illustrated recipes please visit our our site, *They Draw & Cook* (theydrawandcook.com).

Play along by illustrating your own favorite recipe and submitting it to *They Draw & Cook*.

We are easy to find and fun to follow on Facebook, Twitter, Instagram and Pinterest, too!

Made in the USA
Lexington, KY
27 November 2014